WIN THE MOMENT

WIN THOSE CRITICAL, DEFINING MOMENTS THAT MAY COME ONLY ONCE!

WIN THE MOMENT

WIN THOSE CRITICAL, DEFINING MOMENTS THAT MAY COME ONLY ONCE!

**BY
MIKE JONES**

Copyright ©2018 by Mike Jones

All Rights Reserved. No part of this publication may be reproduced in any form, except for brief quotations in reviews, without the written permission of the publisher.

Printed in the United States of America

Cover and interior design by Jared VanLeuven

ISBN: 978-0-9833305-2-3

DEDICATION

This book is dedicated to the Game Changer Tribe. These are individuals who are committed to altering the future in a positive way and have inspired me through their stories to shamelessly share my gifts with the world and make it a better place because of me. I am grateful for each Game Changer.

TABLE OF CONTENTS

Introduction 9

CHAPTER 1
    Winning Not Whining 13

CHAPTER 2
    Break The Pattern 23

CHAPTER 3
    Capture The Moment 35

CHAPTER 4
    What is The Moment? 41

CHAPTER 5
    What is a Win? 59

CHAPTER 6
    Be Selfish 69

CHAPTER 7
    Defining Moments 77

CHAPTER 8
    I Can't Afford It! 85

INTRODUCTION

After spending over three decades working with people, helping individuals grow personally and professionally, after working with individuals on teams all over the world, helping them to be more productive and create more positive cultures at work and at home, I continue to be amazed at the number of people that operate their lives on autopilot. As a result of being on autopilot, when the slightest circumstance occurs that is out of the ordinary, many of them will experience a bad moment, milk it all day and turn that bad moment into a bad day.

So many people have prescribed ways of dealing with everything that happens in their lives. They have predisposed ways of handling issues, celebrating milestones and victories, mindlessly following the course that others have charted before them. We adhere to traditional ways of being in a relationship, acknowledging the people in our lives and managing our entire life journey.

When we recognize that there are 86,400 moments in every day, when we understand that every one of those moments presents an opportunity to live and not just exist, that's when we take our life from autopilot to full throttle. Every moment offers us a gift to play to win rather than simply play not to lose.

When we can clearly accept that we own every one of those moments, that we are not victims to them, and that our choices are creating our realities, our life will be transformed forever.

Research has shown and personal experience has revealed that small steps will get us to big outcomes. One of the keys is consistently moving in the same direction, while remaining focused on a specific outcome.

Creating a life changing new habit is difficult to do, however, taking small steps and winning the moment is within all of your capabilities. I am encouraging you to make a commitment to yourself to "Just do WIT" (Whatever It Takes) in the moment, and *Win the Moment*.

CHAPTER 1
WINNING NOT WHINING

Several months ago a few of my team members and many of my clients suggested that I write another book. I agreed it was time because I had a ton of topics and ideas in my head that I knew would help people, so I began using my new form of note-taking to capture my thoughts, the Notes app on my iPhone.

After months of coaching sessions and conducting training classes with Discover Leadership Training, one book title kept emerging to the top of the list, *Win the Moment*. I found myself saying this over and over to others and even to myself. I developed a morning affirmation: I am courageous enough to risk success and I am unified both within myself and with those to whom I choose to give my love. I will win the moment. I will win the day.

Every day that passed after making the decision on the title, I jotted down notes in my iPhone Notes app, and I also captured experiences that would be great stories for this new book. You may be asking, "Mike, where is this going? Why should I care?" Well, I am glad you asked. Please read on, there is a reason I am telling you this story.

The Time Had Come

My team had publicized a completion date for this new book, however, I missed the deadline. I was not ready mentally or spiritually to write the book. This book was going to be special and it could be my last. I knew this book would benefit thousands of people, even after I died.

With my outcome in mind to make this book special and relevant, I took extra time to record every thought and capture every moment that would make this book significant.

About mid-June 2017, I went on a fishing trip to Devils Lake, ND with two friends, Dan Pforr and Dan Kadrmas from True North Steel. After spending some contemplative, beautiful moments on the lake and capturing a few more thoughts in my Notes app, I decided it was finally time to write this book.

On the last night at Devils Lake, ND I called my wife Susan, told her about my day and I announced to her that it was time; I was ready to write this book. We talked about a plan to give me the space and time to get started.

The game plan was that I would get up daily at 3:30 a.m. and complete as much of my "8 B4 8" as I could before sitting down to write. (You will learn more about developing your own 8 B4 8 in Chapter 2.)

We decided that after I completed the book outline and content we would evaluate whether I would travel somewhere to put the final polish on it.

When I arrived home from my fishing trip, Susan had cleaned my home office and placed a scented candle there. She shared her thoughts on how I could start my mornings to get into a clear mind-set to begin this book and we agreed on a schedule.

The Ultimate Punch In The Gut

On Friday, June 30, 2017, the day after I returned from Fargo, Susan and I got up at 4:00 a.m., began our 8 B4 8, which included going on a 2.5 mile walk. Before I left for my fishing trip with Dan and Dan, I conducted one of our 4-day Master Graduate Leadership Programs (MGLP) and at the conclusion of the program I flew to Fargo, ND before I had shared the experience of the MGLP with Susan.

All of the stories from that 4-day MGLP and the 3 days of fishing provided a lot of rich things to talk about during our early morning walk. The conversation was so rich that I stopped a few times and entered notes on my iPhone. After the walk, we got ready for the day and headed in to the office. I planned to convert the notes into a bestselling book as soon as I woke up the next morning.

Saturday morning arrived and the time had come! I was ready to begin writing this book, a book that would help people live life to win, not whine.

I awoke at 3:30 a.m., turned on my computer and had my iPhone in hand to begin pulling months of thoughts, ideas and years of experience together to write this book. I clicked on the Notes app on the iPhone, the place I'd been jotting down every 'aha' moment, every awareness that came to me, every thought that would make a great point over the last few months – AND THEY WERE GONE. The specific page within the Notes app for my *Win the Moment* notes was not even there. There had to be a good reason for this, had the Russians hacked my iPhone Notes? Where could they have possibly gone?

I sat at the desk in my home office paralyzed, feeling like I had just been punched in the gut by a heavy weight fighter. I closed my eyes and said to myself as I had to many others over the years, "There is nothing wrong, nothing is broken and nothing needs to be fixed, in this present moment there is a universal conspiracy going on and it is focused on my success, *Win the Moment*, Mike Jones."

Just do WIT (Whatever It Takes)

I opened my eyes, I felt strong, ready to "Just do WIT" (Whatever It Takes) to recapture as many of my thoughts as possible. I was ready to win, not whine about everything I had lost. In that moment I asked myself, "Where do I begin?" The response that came back was, "With what you have and what you know."

I immediately began writing. I asked (as you will see), "What is the Moment?" and I wrote for the next hour and a half. When Susan woke up, I shared with her that I had somehow lost my book notes and that the page within the Notes app disappeared. We went out for a 2.5 mile run/walk and talked about potential solutions to recover the lost data. You see, in a small business everyone wears multiple hats. Susan was the in-house attorney, the Operations Vice President, and most importantly in this moment, the IT person for Discover Leadership Training.

> *I am courageous enough to risk success and I am unified both within myself and with those to whom I choose to give my love. I will win the moment. I will win the day.*

I was so anxious after our walk that all I could think of was the possibility of recovering the lost data. Susan had some great ideas and found some potential solutions on Google. I was even more eager to execute this possible resolve to recover my lost data. As soon as breakfast was over, Susan got her computer and we went to work. I hovered over her, constantly questioning why she was doing it that way and giving her suggestions on how to do it to speed up the process. She became frustrated with me and I was clearly not helping, so I decided to leave the room.

I sat in my office waiting for the big win, the loud cheer, fireworks, *something*, however, it never came. She did everything just as outlined on the Apple website to recover the data yet it did not produce the result we wanted.

We hammered out a few more ways to change our approach to get to our outcome of recovering the data. We decided I would take the phone to the Apple store in the neighborhood; however, it did not open until 10:00 a.m. Susan and I previously scheduled a marketing meeting with Antoine and Kyoko Hicks of Events by Eclectic in our home at 10:30 a.m. I asked Susan if she thought I could be at the Apple store when it opened and be back for the meeting once they recovered my Notes.

Of course, she said no, and I needed to respect my commitment to be here for the Hicks meeting. I agreed, even though I so badly wanted to be in my car headed to the Apple store to figure out how to find my Notes. This was a big deal to me, and now I truly believed in the possibility that the Notes could be recovered.

As I remained committed to winning not whining, I decided to call the Apple store to see if they could help me recover the data over the phone. I called Apple at 10:00 a.m. and went through several different approaches with the Apple team member to recover the data. I was even more hopeful now as he diagnosed the problem and further looked into recovering many months of content for my book.

After 30 minutes he asked for my phone number and said that he would talk to a few members of his team to see if they could figure out a solution. He said he would call me back in one hour and thirty minutes. I felt disappointed in that moment and I felt anxiousness creeping back in again.

Would You Like Some Cheese With That Whine?

By this time, Antoine and Kyoko Hicks had arrived and were being greeted by Susan as I finished my call. As soon as I got off the phone with the Apple store, I threw up all over the Hicks about losing my Notes. I did the unthinkable for me; I was selling tickets to my pity party. I was whining.

As I told them what occurred, I remembered reading my daily positive message at 3:30 a.m. before beginning the writing process. The message for July 1st came from the book I wrote in 2015 entitled *365 Powerful, Positive Thoughts To Start Your Day*.

The positive thought for July 1st read: You have likely received, and perhaps sent out a few invitations to some pity parties. I promise you they are no fun and attending a pity party will only produce a negative outcome. Now that you have that awareness, my coaching to you is to not waste your time and energy feeling sorry for yourself and others because it will never benefit anyone.

The sooner you refocus on your positive outcome, the sooner this party will become a celebration. It is PARTY TIME!! I am Positive!

I am not kidding, that really happened. You cannot make this up. So, I withdrew the tickets to my pity party and declared that whether I was able to recover those Notes or not, this book will be written and it will be amazing.

I looked at Kyoko and she had this look in her eyes. She asked a few questions, grabbed her computer and started looking for a solution. Before I knew it the pity party ended and every one of them were engaged in finding a solution. Susan was on the phone with our IT provider, Kyoko was changing her approach again and again. Antoine was asking probing questions that created new possibilities.

It's Not Over, Until You Say It Is Over

About one hour and fifteen minutes later, Kyoko found the solution and recovered the lost data. Indeed a celebration ensued, high fives, hugs and a toast. Oh my God, I was so overcome with gratitude. Wow, look at what happens when you put a group of people together, focused on a positive outcome, in the midst of a challenging situation.

When you have a choice to win or whine, choose to win. When you have a choice to be positive or negative, choose positive and Win the Moment. When you have a choice to be a victim or to be victorious, choose to be victorious. Win the Moment by accepting personal responsibility to remain focused on what you want and continue to Win the Moment as you change your approach to change your results until you get what you want. I know this can sometimes be challenging, however, keep fighting through the challenge for what you want.

I often tell people, having negative thoughts does not make you a negative person, executing the negative thoughts into actions will define you as a negative person. Remaining focused on what you want is one of the keys to winning.

When I say this to clients I have coached, the response I sometimes receive is, "I don't know what I want or I don't know where I want to go". When you see that as your truth, you are selling tickets to your pity party. You have taken on the role of a victim. The biggest realization I want you to have right now is you are lying to yourself. Now hold on, there is no need to throw this book against the wall; stick with me and continue reading with the intent to be influenced to bigger wins.

It is impossible to say you don't know what you want or you don't know where you want to go because if you didn't know, you would not know that you didn't know.

So let's stop for a moment and do a little work. Grab a pen and some paper or perhaps the Notes app on your mobile device and answer these questions for yourself:

- What do you want to do with your life?
- Where are you going professionally and personally?
- Why are you here on this earth?
- What do you want to accomplish in your life?
- What do you stand for?

For some of you, answering these questions will be difficult, because it requires you to be honest with yourself; it requires you to take personal responsibility for your life. If you are ready to start winning and stop whining, then *Win the Moment* by having the courage to take a stand and declare what you want.

WIN THE MOMENT

CHAPTER 2
BREAK THE PATTERN

Many times when I say to my clients that in order to create sustainable change, you must break your old patterns, they respond by saying, "I have been doing the things I do this way for a long time. Where do I begin to start breaking the old patterns?" My answer to them is that it is always best to start at the beginning.

Let's begin by breaking the pattern of how you start your day. Here is a gift I give to people who attend our programs and to the members of the Game Changer Tribe*; a process I call "8 B4 8". This is a list of 8 essential things you will make a commitment to do before 8:00 a.m. in your time zone for the next 30 days. These 8 tasks should be things that are 100% within your control. You can categorize these things as Professional and Personal. Each of these things should be meaningful to you and give you a sense of accomplishment once you have completed them.

Here are just a few examples to consider adding to your list of 8 B4 8:

- Read something positive
- Get in a workout
- Have a morning party, turn on some upbeat positive music
- Spend quality time with your significant other

- Call your parents
- Affirm something positive about yourself
- Complete a WIT (Whatever It Takes) List for your day
- Eat a healthy meal
- Drink a specific amount of water
- Meditate/Pray
- Go for a morning run
- Write an article
- Connect with a specific number of your clients
- Connect with a friend
- Go for a bike ride
- Catch someone doing something right
- Organize your house
- Wake your children gently
- Plan your meals for the day
- Take a long relaxing shower

Although it is ideal to be consistent, I caution you to not have an attachment to always completing your list of 8 B4 8. This is not offering you an excuse to not follow through; it is the awareness that from time to time things happen that may prevent you from completing all the tasks on your list.

If you had "run 3 miles" on your list and there is a thunderstorm in your area that morning, you may want to skip the run and find an alternate way to complete your cardio.

When you begin your day with 8 B4 8, you will have a higher level of focus, engagement, positivity, and a sense of accomplishment every day. If you make a commitment and follow through with your 8 B4 8 for a minimum of 30 days, everything that occurs during your day will be systemically affected and you will find old patterns fade away. My coaching is to start at the beginning.

I have taught people that words create pictures. Have you ever wondered where the patterns, beliefs and behaviors that you have come from?

Think back to your early years with your parents or in school; the adult in your life showed you a picture of something and then gave you an identifying word by saying, "This picture represents a dog." You looked at the picture and you repeated the word, "dog". Then the adult showed you a picture of a cat, or a horse and gave you the identifying word and you would repeat it. The adult had you do this until you could pick out each animal and properly identify them.

Repetitiously practicing a behavior allows you to develop a habit or pattern you can execute with little or no thought. Getting into a pattern and consistently following through with anything, whether good or bad, will develop muscle memory. Develop your 8 B4 8 to build muscle around a positive start to your day.

Are You a Chump or a Champion?

You have often heard people say, "Practice makes perfect" and they are correct. If you practice something over and over again, you will perfectly deliver it the same way. That does not imply that you are performing the task at an effective high level. It means that the way you practice is the way you will play at game time.

If you practice like a chump, you will perfectly deliver like a chump at game time. If you practice like a champion, you will perfectly deliver like a champion at game time.

We could spend a lot of time uncovering what you were taught or what you were not taught from other human beings. We could talk about the patterns and disciplines of the people who taught you or the lack there of, however, you are in control of you now. In fact, you are authentically the only thing you have control over. Therefore, whatever has happened to you, happened. You are now the boss, and you have the power and authority to create the person you want to be.

The time has come to break the pattern of how you treat yourself and others. Okay… stop that, you know what I am talking about. I did not say that you treat yourself and others poorly. I never said there was anything wrong, broken or that needed to be fixed; what I said was there is an opportunity to identify and break your present patterns and create an even better version of yourself.

Let's be clear about something before we begin this work, if someone else's opinion of you has you feeling like a champion or a chump, you are destined to fail. If the opinions of others have you feeling like a champion, when they become upset with you, or you do not fulfill their expectations of you, they will change their opinion and you will become a chump.

In order to become a champion in whatever professional capacity you have chosen, you must practice like a champion. In order to become a champion as a partner, parent or friend, you must practice like a champion. One of the best moments to evaluate whether you are a chump or a champion is when you get pushed out of your comfort zone or a crisis occurs. Do you typically have a knee-jerk reaction or do you provide a contemplative response?

If you unconsciously react, it is mindless behavior. It is based off of the actions you have practiced over and over. When you react this way, you will produce a predictable future. Now some of you may feel that you play at a high level and as you judge yourself and your successes based on a comparison to others, you may erroneously feel your reaction will produce a champion outcome. I submit when you get pushed out of your comfort zone, your reaction to the circumstance is focused generally on survival. This is the chump approach.

When you reflectively respond after being pushed out of your comfort zone, you are poised and calm. You know where your response will lead you. When you respond after reflecting it will likely be deliberate and confident and you will produce a brand new future. Your response to a specific outcome will likely create an outcome focused on thriving. This is the champion approach.

WIN THE MOMENT

You are a chump if:

- You make excuses the moment something goes wrong
- You are waiting for someone to give you permission to live
- You do not feel that you are worthy of the best things in life
- Your team or family must overcome your negativity in order to succeed
- You see the glass half empty
- You are not growing as a person everyday
- You make judgements of people based on the 1% of them visible to you, their appearance
- You make people wrong, just so you get to be right
- You take from others
- You are not patient with the people in your life
- You break your word
- You do good nuf' just to get through something
- You go along with the crowd
- You give more value to someone else than you do yourself
- You care more about what others think of you than what you think of yourself

Clearly this list could go on; however, I am sure you get the point.

You are a champion if:

- You accept personal responsibility for everything going on in your life

- You are living your life on purpose

- You know you are worthy of everything you want from life

> *You will not need willpower to Win the Moment, all you will need is a commitment to your outcome.*

- You are a part of the positive environment that is allowing your team and family to succeed

- You see the glass half full

- You are making the choice to grow personally everyday

- You take the time to get to know people from the inside out

- You realize you do not have to make others wrong in order for you to be right

- You give to others

- You demonstrate patience and empathy to the people in your life

- You have integrity with your word

- You give 100% everyday

- You fully understand why you made the choice you made
- You see the good in yourself
- You are independent of the opinions of others

Again, clearly this list could go on; however, I am sure you get the point. You were not born a chump or a champion. The behaviors that you have been practicing have created your reality.

Small Steps, Small Wins

It does not matter if you see yourself as a chump or a champion in this moment, our focus is on getting to your next level of development. Let's take a look at how you can break whatever pattern you have established.

The game plan as we break the pattern and win the moment will be on small steps to get small wins. As we take small steps or micro steps we progress and trend in the direction that will produce the positive outcomes we are focused on. Sometimes these "small steps" are referred to as micro steps because the steps need to be very focused. This will be more of a rifle approach rather than a shot gun approach.

As we get small wins, a compilation of those small wins, will equal a big win. It has been said that Rome was not built in a day and neither were you. You have been building the you that exists in this moment over the number of years you have been on this earth.

As we focus on breaking the pattern, make a commitment to

a 30-day challenge. I call this a "challenge" because on some level this may be an undertaking for you. Be aware that the greatest challenge will come from within you. Nothing that has occurred in your life has made you the person you are today. As I stated earlier, your reaction or response to what was occurring made the difference.

When you reacted, that was knee-jerk, thoughtless and focused on survival. When you responded, it was thoughtful, and generally focused on a specific outcome.

Our focus will not be on any of your past failures, we will not focus on how much willpower or discipline you have or do not have. Our focus is on winning the moment. The game plan will be on small steps, small wins. You will not need willpower or discipline to win the moment, all you need is a commitment to your outcome. Now I don't care who you are, that is some Smokin' Hottt Shit.

Here is a question I have for you as you begin this 30-day challenge. Would you rather suffer the pain of commitment or the pain of regret? One lasts for a moment, the other last all day and sometimes beyond. I encourage you to treat each moment as if you were taking the winning shot. What will determine how many of those shots you hit will be the choices you make in those moments. If the choice is focused on what happened yesterday, you will likely miss the shot. Yesterday is a closed, locked door and the key has been thrown away. You cannot go back there.

In order to hit the winning shot, you must make the right choice in the moment, no matter how tough or uncomfortable it is for you to make that choice. The way for you to be crystal clear that the choice you need to make is the right one, is determined by the positive outcome you are focused on. As you focus on that outcome, take the small step necessary and *Win the Moment*.

You will need to bring a few things with you to the playing field during this 30-day challenge in order to ensure your success. These are things that are available to you in this moment. You need to set a specific outcome, identify the benefits of reaching that outcome, affirm your commitment to it, and become consistent in practicing the new behaviors.

Okay, so our outcome for this 30-day challenge will be to create new behavioral patterns. The benefit will be to create a better version of you.

Here is all I am asking you to do for 30 days consecutively.

- Get up 10 minutes earlier than normal. I did not say wake up 10 minutes earlier, I said, "Get up." Our focus is to break the pattern and create a new normal. There will be unintended positive results from doing this if you are consistent for the entire 30 days. When the alarm goes off, you must *Win the Moment*. Come on, you've got this.

- Next, write this down on paper, "Anything that can possibly go right today, will go right." It's not okay to write it once and read it for 30 days. You need to write it down each day. As soon as you get up, get a piece of paper and write it down. Take these small steps, and let's get a few quick small wins.

- As we take the next small step, I want you to drink a minimum of 8 ounces of water. Once again, if you are consistent you will see unintended positive, systemic benefits in other areas of your life. Now I said water, not juice, coffee or an energy drink.

- At the end of your day, before you go to bed, write down one thing that went right that day. Don't judge how big or small it was, just capture one thing that went right every day for the 30-day time period. I know some of you will freak out if we call this a journal or diary, so let's not. Let's just call it the little book or file in the Notes app on your phone where you are recording a note every day. Make a commitment to take this small step daily for 30 days.

Unintended Positive Results

In order to successfully break the pattern, you will need to trust the process and make a commitment to do this every day. Perform each of these activities consistently. If you create a conversation with yourself that this is too hard, then that simply means the benefits from doing this work are not greater than the benefits of staying where you are.

When you make the commitment to take this on, there will be several unintended positive results. This is an opportunity to practice like a champion, taking small steps, micro steps and getting small wins.

Once you have completed this, you will see the value and begin applying this process to other things in your life such as, successfully implementing a daily workout program, eating healthier, stop smoking, improving your relationships, increasing your marketability, becoming a better parent, or growing personally.

Quite often when people are focused on breaking old patterns, they attempt to do too much, too fast. Teaching yourself to take small steps and getting small wins will allow you to push past your fears, change your perceptions, breakthrough past limitations and *Win the Moment* as you create new patterns. Let's do this!

*Discover Leadership Trainings definition of a Game Changer is the individual that is altering a negative future in a positive way. The Game Changer Tribe is a group of individuals both graduates and non-graduates of our programs. The only requirement to be a member of the Game Changer Tribe is a commitment to create more positivity in your home and at your place of business.

CHAPTER 3
CAPTURE THE MOMENT

Yogi Berra was a Major League Baseball player for the New York Yankees from 1949-1963. He was a very colorful character that played, managed, and coached in the MLB for over 19 years.

Yogi Berra often coined quotes that would make you stop and think for a moment. One of my favorite quotes from him is, "When you come to a fork in the road, take it." The awareness is one moment later the opportunity will not be the same. What I am touching on here is optimizing the moment. We have heard people say, "There is no time like the present." Wow, I am not sure they know how profound and powerful that statement is.

When you come to a fork in the road, you will need to be decisive. You must have the courage to take action now. Every one of those forks will be like a footstep. Doing nothing, standing still, or going straight in this context is not available to you. In this moment, you will need to go right or left. Whichever direction you choose will lead you somewhere; the only way to be sure it is leading you where you want to go is by making a decision about it ahead of time. What is your outcome?

The Fork in the Road

If I have not taken the time to determine where I am going, then I am playing the game based on chance. This does not mean

I do not *know* what I want. Rather, it generally means, I have not had the courage to *declare* what I want.

If you know where you are going, when you come to the fork in the road, you will know which way to turn to continue moving, progressing, and trending in the right direction.

If I am playing the game based on chance, I am living my life *hoping* it turns out okay, generally celebrating someone else's pain in an effort to feel like I didn't lose. Have you heard yourself or others make statements like, "Well, I don't have it as bad as..." or "It could always be worse"? That is just another way of saying I did not lose as bad as someone else did. Let's get crystal clear about something, celebrating someone else's pain is not gain for you and not losing does not mean you won.

There will continue to be ebbs and flows, ups and downs in our economic stability. When you come to that fork in the road, the economic climate will not determine your financial success. You must capture that moment by remaining focused on where you are going. The fork in the road may provide you with an opportunity to change your approach to get to the results you want. The sooner you capture that moment, the more you will optimize the positive results available to you. It is important to note that if you take a wrong turn, it is not fatal, however, the sooner you recognize it was the wrong turn and turn around, the better.

> *My coaching to you is to capture that moment. If you see that moment as wrong, unfair, or negative, you will have made a wrong turn.*

You will continue to come to forks in the road in your professional life. Many of these forks, circumstances, barriers and obstacles will be things you have no control over. You must capture those moments as many of them will only come once. It does not matter if you are the CEO of the company or in an entry level position, you will experience some forks in the road. They will come in the form of lost contracts, unhappy customers, dishonest employees, a negative boss, an unfair manager, a natural disaster or an inappropriate decision. It will not matter what resources you have when you get to this fork in the road; what will matter is how resourceful you are.

My coaching to you is to capture that moment. If you see that moment as wrong, unfair, or negative, you will have made a wrong turn. When you come to a fork in the road, you are presented with an opportunity to authenticate where you are going. Ignoring that moment will not be fatal; however, you will not be able to capture the optimal benefit because you created a negative you must first overcome.

There will be forks in the road in your personal relationships. The way you have dealt with those forks in the past, is determining how you deal with the forks in the road you are experiencing now. Be willing to break the pattern and change your approach if you want different results.

I often ask people I coach, "What do you really want out of a relationship?" Quite often I get the exact same vague response; they say, "I want to be happy." Simply stating to someone that you want to be happy is the most dangerous statement you can make.

Here is an awareness for you, you just gave someone permission to treat you in such a way that defines happy to them. That very likely will not make you happy. You think that buffoon should know what you mean when you say, "I want to be happy." So you continue to be unhappy, because they only know their definition of "make you happy".

The Best Way to Get What You Want

Okay, I am not a mind reader, however, I am going to predict that some of you are thinking we all should know and live by the Golden Rule which says, "Treat me the way you want me to treat you." This is as dangerous as simply telling someone that what you want out of the relationship is to be happy.

I learned in my many years of personal coaching with clients, there are people that do not want to be treated the way you want to be treated. Even more important, the definition of what I want is likely different from the definition others have of the same thing. If I say, "Having a supportive partner will make me happy," the person I am with has their own definition of what it means to be supportive and that needs to be identified. If I never clearly explain to them what my definition is, they will support me according to their definition and I will continue to be unhappy because they are not a supportive partner to me.

What I meant by supportive was I wanted my partner to have dinner on the table when I get home and to take my clothes to the laundry every week. What my partner meant by supportive is that I would stay home with the baby twice a week and help with the household chores every day.

I do not care how long you have been with someone; they cannot read your mind. They may get lucky sometimes after watching your patterns and listening to you rant in your unhappiness, however, the fastest, most effective way to get what you want from your partner is to tell them what you want and need from them.

How will you know what they need from you if you never ask? It will only take one of you to step up to break the pattern and completely change the game. Why not you? Immediately, some of you will start whining about what you have already "tried" to do in your relationship. If what you have done did not produce the results you wanted, you must be willing to change your approach. You can continue whining or you can start winning.

When we are not getting the things from our partner that we need, we blame our partner for not making us happy. My question to you is how will they ever authentically know your definition of supportive, intimate, loving, effective communicator, best friend, have my back, great partner if you never tell them your definition?

When you come to that relational fork in the road, my coaching is to capture that moment by living according to the Platinum Rule: Treat me the way I want to be treated. They will not be able to deliver that unless you tell them what you want and need from them.

This is Your Now

Every fork in the road will present a positive turn and a negative turn. Every fork in the road will present an opportunity for you to trend to where you want to go and the opportunity to trend away from where you want to go.

When you come to a fork in the road and you choose to procrastinate, have a piss poor attitude, have an I don't give a damn attitude, blame others, feel like a victim, feel you have no choice, or quit, you took a wrong turn.

Every choice you make at the fork in the road is going to matter. If a negative thought arises when you get to the fork in the road, no big deal. If you allow the negative thought to determine which direction you choose, then that choice will have defined your direction.

Knowing where I am going allows me to capture the moment; it allows me to be bold, self-confident, enthusiastic, focused, determined, passionate and deliberate. Capturing the moment allows me to *Win the Moment*.

CHAPTER 4
WHAT IS THE MOMENT?

"Live in the present. Launch yourself on each wave. Find eternity in each moment."

Henry David Thoreau

"The foolish man seeks happiness in the distance; the wise grows it under his feet."

James Oppenheim

What is the moment? The moment is time. There are 86,400 seconds in each day. Every one of them represents a moment in the context of this conversation. It doesn't matter who you are, it is an absolute fact, we have ALL been given the same amount of time every day.

The realities you experienced in your life are the result of how you chose to spend each of those moments. There are many of you who attribute the circumstances you have experienced in life as the reason you are winning or losing your moments. I want to be clear early in this book, in the context of this conversation, you are not a victim. I submit that one of the greatest gifts every one of us has is the gift of choice.

The Future is NOW

I have often heard people say to pre-teens, teenagers and

young adults, that they are the future. Ladies and gentlemen, this is erroneous thinking because they are not the future; they are the NOW. The choices they are making right now are winning or losing the moment: the choice to make excuses or accept personal responsibility, the choice to go for what they want or blame others for preventing them from getting what they say they want, the choice to take action now and Just do WIT (Whatever It Takes) to be successful or be lazy and procrastinate, and the choice to judge the value of a person based on gender, color of skin, religion, or sexual preference rather than character and work ethic. The choices they are making in this moment will shape and develop who they will become. It is occurring right NOW.

Every Moment Matters

During a visit to Los Angeles, CA to conduct a training class for a team I was working with, I was sitting in the hotel restaurant eating breakfast. As I observed all the people at breakfast, I became crystal clear why there is so much obesity, diabetes, heart disease and cancer in the U.S. Now I am not going to lecture you on what is right for you, I leave that choice for you to make. I just want to turn the lights on and have you open your eyes to see what is occurring in the moment because every moment matters.

The moment you are living in right now is creating your future. In this situation, your future health and the health of your children are within your care, custody and control. Did what you just put in your body trend you towards good health or bad health? Did it just trend towards life or death? Did you just win that moment regarding your health? Do you have a specific, positive outcome regarding your health?

WHAT IS THE MOMENT?

Every moment matters, and there are 86,400 of them in a 24-hour day. The choice that you make in this moment will positively trend you toward good health or poor health. Before putting anything in your body, know you are at choice.

When addressing this with people I conduct 1:1 coaching with, I often hear things like, "We are all going to die of something." Okay, that is true, however, let this be an awareness of how you are playing the game. When the game is over (and yes, it will end one day for every one of us), I submit it will not matter what your final score is. What will matter is how you played the game.

Is the way you play the game regarding your health creating the potential of more healthy moments for you to spend with your significant other, family and friends?

This is a conversation about what you have control of, a conversation about being a healthy role model, a conversation about saying "thank you" to God and your parents for the greatest gift you will ever receive and that gift is your life. This is not the moment to blame your parents or anyone else for the unhealthy eating habits they may have role modeled for you. This is the moment to break the pattern. This is the moment to take control of your life. This is the moment to accept personal responsibility for the choice you just made because that choice will matter.

Some of you are over halfway through your lives and others of you are at the end of your lives, and you don't even know it. All that you have is the moment you are presently experiencing and this moment matters. Live it full out.

You Are The Creator

None of us came into this world with a hardwire to be the person that we are today or the person we have the potential of becoming in the future. The choices you make in this moment are creating that person. I don't care who you are, that is a Smokin' Hottt awareness. No matter the color of your skin, your gender, your sexual preference or what your religious beliefs are, you have free will as a gift. You are always at choice. The gift of choice allows you the opportunity to be whomever you choose to be.

Oh yes, I am talking to you. This is true for you also; the choice you make in this moment is creating your reality. A circumstance is a circumstance and in some instances, multiple people will be experiencing the exact same situation and due to their choices, will experience a different reality than others. As soon as you accept that level of personal responsibility, everything will change. You will win the moment and the whining and making excuses will cease.

Choose Wisely

I was in Houston, TX in August 2017 when hurricane Harvey slammed into the Gulf Coast. There were lives lost and unprecedented property damage due to historical flooding. This was a massive circumstance that was affecting millions of people directly and indirectly, ALL at the same time. I learned early in my life that having knowledge means that you know what to do, having wisdom means you know when to do it.

WHAT IS THE MOMENT?

There were so many moments won and lost based on the choices people were making in the moment; the choice to heed the warnings and evacuate or the choice to hunker down. The choice to drive through flooded streets or the choice to turn around. These were moments that became life and death situations. Some of these moments were won and some of these moments were lost.

In the aftermath of hurricane Harvey, the choice points continued. Do I remain in this flooded house or do I move to higher ground in a shelter? The rising flood waters were another circumstance affecting multiple people at the same time. Some of those affected won the moment by choosing to heed the warnings and leave, while others lost the moment by choosing to stay.

> I was unfazed by his news about what was realistic or normal.

Ready Or Not, Here I Come

Hurricane Harvey was a massive circumstance. This storm did not ask anyone for permission to affect their lives the way it did. Harvey did not pause to ask what race the people that were affected by its winds, water or storm surge was. It did not pause to ask, "Is this a rich or poor neighborhood?" Harvey did not ask, "What are the religious beliefs of the people affected by my fury?"

Hurricane Harvey showed up on ALL of our door steps. It did not ask permission to blow your house down. Harvey did not ask permission to flood your house and car. It did not judge or discriminate in any way. He simply said, "Ready or not, here

I come."

Whatever reality we experienced during and after hurricane Harvey was based on our individual choices regarding the challenging circumstances the storm created.

The reality of how we recovered and moved forward as individuals was also the result of the choices we made. It is my wish for you, when you go through circumstances that are life changing, you do not focus on restoring calm or normal.

Many circumstances push us out of our comfort zone and provide us with an opportunity to create something brand new. The circumstance provides us with an opportunity to get to another level and often offers us an opportunity to *Win the Moment*. If we blame the circumstance for the reality we are experiencing, the game is over for us. When you accept personal responsibility for the choices you make regarding the circumstance, Game On for you baby!

If I Were You

We are all faced with many different circumstances to deal with on our life's journey. Dan Kadrmas, Dan Pforr and I had some very rich conversations during my fishing trip to Devils Lake. As we talked, I was reminded we ALL have different perspectives. We can only evaluate the circumstances others are experiencing through our own experiences and belief system. Have you ever shared a circumstance you were going through with someone and they said, "If I were you, I would…." and they proceeded to give you advice based on their perspective that would never work for you?

Some of you were born with a silver spoon in your mouth; others were born with a wooden spoon. Some of you went to private school, some went to public school, others were home schooled. Some of you are considered tall and others short. Some of you have blonde hair and blue eyes, some have no hair. Some of you have fair skin and others dark skin. Some of you had amazing parents and role models in your lives and others had horrible parents and negative role models. Some of you are athletic and others sedentary. Some of you are thin and others fat. Some of you would be considered physically attractive and others not attractive at all.

None of the above gets to determine whether you are valuable or not valuable. None of the above will determine if you will be successful or a failure. In fact, none of the above will determine your worth as a human being, because none of the above is true. Truth or lies in this present moment is determined by you; no one gets to define you without your permission to do so. Only your agreement makes what others say about you true.

Read over the last two paragraphs again and be aware that none of it is good or bad, right or wrong, positive or negative; only your thinking makes it so. All of it is based on personal assessments and relative comparisons resulting from someone's perspective.

Now that is some more Smokin' Hottt Shit and if you can truly embrace that awakening and awareness, your life is about to be transformed forever.

Unfazed By Your Truth

When I first began this journey of personal growth and self-exploration over 30 years ago, I was working with teenagers in Houston area high schools. As a Houston Police Helicopter Pilot, I developed a program named Soul Patrol. You may have just asked yourself why I named the program Soul Patrol. Well, I am so glad you asked. It was not because of my ethnicity or because the program was focused on Black at-risk teenagers. The Soul Patrol Program was designed and presented to all teenagers without regard to the color of their skin or their socio-economic status. I recognized that all of these teens were dealing with a lot of the same issues.

When I joined the Houston Police Department, I did so with the intention of going to the Helicopter Division and flying the police helicopter. After watching the police chase people through my neighborhood as a young boy, I often dreamed of flying that helicopter.

As I went through the interview process, I informed my Houston Police Department recruiter of my intentions of going to the Helicopter Division. The recruiter warned me that the average seniority of a person considered for the Helicopter Division was 10 years of service as a police officer and most people had to apply several times before they were awarded one of those prestigious spots. He said he wanted me to be realistic about my chances of being transferred to the Helicopter Division. You need to be aware that you cannot share your dreams with everyone.

I was unfazed by his news about what was realistic or normal. I completed the recruiting process and was sent to the

Police Academy for 16 weeks. After completing that process, I was sent to the Patrol Division at the Beechnut substation, then the Jail Division, and then back to the Beechnut substation. Soon after, a spot opened in the Helicopter Division and I was so excited. I applied for the position even though I was told by my supervisors it was a waste of time because I had not been on the police department long enough to be considered for a transfer to the Helicopter Division. I was unfazed by the historical data they were sharing with me. I chose not to allow it to shape my belief about what was possible.

Out of hundreds of applicants, I was granted an interview. I arrived at the interview dressed in my blue police uniform and sat before a panel of sergeants assigned to the Helicopter Division to answer questions. I was given an opportunity to confidently make a statement of why I was the best applicant for the position in the Helicopter Division. I truly felt like I won the moment. I answered every question with passion and conviction as to why I was the best candidate. I informed the panel that I was already a commercial airplane pilot which equipped me with the knowledge needed for the Helicopter Division and conveyed my enthusiasm and dream of flying for the Houston Police Department.

Time To Write A New Story

After I completed the interview, I was told by a Black officer that I did not stand a chance in hell of being assigned to the Helicopter Division. He told me stories of how many times he applied for a transfer into the elite division unsuccessfully. He went on to tell me that a Black officer had been transferred to the division and was fired after getting into a fight with White officers because they did not want him there. He said he had heard the supervisors and officers in the Helicopter Division were committed to never allow a "nigger" to fly the helicopters.

It was quite disturbing to think these racist, hateful beliefs still existed in 1986, however, I was unfazed by his story and I waited to see if I would be given a second interview. A few weeks later the call came. I made the cut and was given a second interview.

Again, I arrived in my police dress uniform, met with sergeants and the division lieutenant and confidently answered more questions. At the conclusion of the interview, they stated they would make their selection in a few weeks.

After my second interview, my division captain called me into his office and said he heard I was clearly the most qualified officer for the position; however, they were not selecting me because I was too big for their training helicopter. At that time, I was 6 feet 4 1/2 inches tall and weighed 250 pounds. He further informed me they felt the safety of the training helicopter would be at risk with me and their present flight instructors because of the weight and balance restrictions of the aircraft.

I was unfazed by this information. I was already a commercial airplane pilot, so I clearly understood weight and balance in aviation terms. I did some research on the types of helicopters the Houston Police Department used as training aircraft. I looked at the weight and balance restrictions for the Hughes 300 helicopter and knew what I needed to do.

I knew I could only do what I had control over. So I chose to

Win the Moment. I knew I had about 3 weeks before the selection was made. I set an outcome to be at 225 pounds in 3 weeks.

It Is Yours If You Want It

I completely changed my diet to egg whites and toast for breakfast, baked chicken and vegetables for lunch and dinner and carrots as my snacks. I only drank water and lots of it. I ran 3 miles at 3:30 a.m. to start my day and another 3 miles at night to end my day. Three weeks later my weight was 220 pounds.

I returned to the helicopter division for what they thought would be my third and final interview. When they came into the room to give me the news that I would not be selected as the newest member of the Houston Police Department Helicopter Division, they were shocked.

The reason for denying me the position I dreamed of most of my life did not exist in that moment. They left the room without letting me know their decision. They returned and informed me that I had been selected as the person to fill the position in the Houston Police Department Helicopter Division. I will never forget that moment. One of the sergeants walked up to me as I was leaving and said, "I am impressed."

What Have I Gotten Myself Into?

When I first reported to the division, I was shocked at the level of negativity I faced after breaking through the historically held barriers to be transferred to this prestigious division.

I was initially placed on day shift during the orientation process. On my first day, my fellow officers were quite unfriendly. Every time I walked into a room, all of the officers would leave and go into another room.

The most senior officers in the division were on day shift, so I thought maybe this was their way of welcoming the rookie. However, I soon found out there was much more to this behavior. After a few days of this, I was transferred to the evening/night shift. At that point, I worked a four-day shift, ten hours per shift. At the start of the evening/night shift, I found these officers were also very unfriendly. Every time I walked into a room, there was a mass exodus.

I was not sure what to make of this; however, I was still happy to be there. I later found out the White officers did not want to fly with me. They paired me up with a Black officer and we flew together more often than not. The White officers named us the "Soul Patrol". There is so much more to this story, however, that is not the purpose of this book.

I could have gotten angry and did something negative and gotten fired like the other Black officer, or I could *Win the Moment*, remain focused on my positive outcome and keep moving forward and that is what I did.

Transforming a Negative to a Positive

It was the mid-1980s and the "Just Say No" campaign was in full swing as part of the United States "War on Drugs". The campaign was enacted to discourage children from engaging in illegal drug use by offering various ways to say "No". As a police officer, I saw a need to address an issue I identified. During the "Just Say No to Drugs" era, I realized that we were telling kids what not to do, rather than what to do.

I developed a program focused on telling kids what to say "Yes" to and the emphasis was on their education. I founded an organization with an outcome to inspire, motivate and empower teenagers to take control of their lives by besting their best and increasing their core course grades by two points each grading period. It was quite successful in Houston and eventually became a nationwide program. Guess what I named it? You got it – Soul Patrol. I made the choice to transform the negative situation my fellow HPD officers created to a positive reality for teenagers across the nation.

I don't care who you are, negative things will happen in your life, however, you can Win the Moment by transforming the negative to a positive. What happens to you does not define you, how you react or respond to it defines you. If you assess situations that occur in your life as bad, negative or wrong, then the energy and action you approach it with will be negative. Please be aware that everything reproduces a likeness of itself.

The officers that called me and my helicopter patrol partner "Soul Patrol" meant it in a racist, negative, derogatory way. I choose to transform it to a positive and as a result, Soul Patrol programs were presented to over four million teenagers in cities across the U.S. during my time at the Houston Police Department. I became one of the most decorated police officers in the State of Texas, had an opportunity to spend a significant amount of time with two U.S. Presidents and also had a long-standing TV show on NBC along with a radio show on Clear Channel radio.

Because I took this negative circumstance and transformed it to a powerful, positive outcome, the officers in the Helicopter Division stopped referring to us as the Soul Patrol.

I encourage you to accept in this moment there will be things that happen to you that will be outside of your control. These things will be barriers to your success; walls that could prevent you from winning. As you go for what you want, as you play full out, negative circumstances will not ask your permission to show up in your life. You may get fired from your job or your business may fail. Be aware that failure is not fatal. Experiencing a break up or going through a divorce can be extremely challenging, however, it is not the end of the world. Losing a loved one is very tough, I know, however, it does not mean that life ends for you.

It is perfectly okay to feel sad, disappointment, or hurt, however, the sooner you transform those situations to something that will produce a positive outcome, the sooner you will win. Now let me be clear about something, I am not suggesting that you get over anything. I am encouraging you to get on with your life. There is a positive available from everything that has happened.

In 1980, Nancy G. Brinker promised her dying sister, Susan, that she would do everything in her power to end breast cancer forever. In 1982, that promise to her sister became the Susan G. Komen® organization and the beginning of a global movement. What was started with $200 and a shoebox full of potential donor names has now grown into the world's largest nonprofit source of funding for the fight against breast cancer. To date, they have invested more than $2.9 billion in groundbreaking research, community health outreach, advocacy and programs in more than 60 countries. Their efforts helped reduce deaths from breast cancer by 38 percent between 1989 and 2014 and they have committed that they will not stop until their promise is fulfilled. Make the choice to consciously respond to negative situations that are occurring in your life rather than a quick knee-jerk reaction. The response will allow you to transform a negative situation to a positive reality for you and the people in your life.

Change Your Approach

In 1850, Nathaniel Hawthorne went home and told his wife that he had just been fired from his job. "Good," she said, "Now you can write your book." "What do we live on meanwhile?" Hawthorne asked. His wife opened a drawer filled with money. "I have always known that you are a man of genius," she said. "So I saved a little each week, and now I have enough to last for a year." Wow, don't you want a partner like that?

Hawthorne used the time to write *The Scarlet Letter*, one of the great masterpieces of American literature. It is a powerful act of courage to transform a negative circumstance into a positive reality.

I later got to meet the Black officer that was fired from the Houston Police Department Helicopter Division for fighting with White officers that were mistreating him. His name is Roscoe Edwards. Roscoe and his wife were a great source of inspiration and support for me as I went through one of the toughest situations I had faced in my life at the HPD Helicopter Division.

I was inspired by how Roscoe also transformed his negative situation to a positive reality by picking himself up after being fired and having his dream snatched away from him. Roscoe dusted himself off and won many moments as he continued to pursue his dream of being a pilot. He became a Captain for Continental Airlines and spent 25 years doing what he loved.

You Are Who You Choose to Be

As human beings, anytime there is something we do not understand, we look for a way to make it make sense by comparing it to something historical. We then apply a label or identity to it which allows us to fit it into our established patterns. The label or identity does not authenticate what this really is or anything else about it. The label or identity simply allows us to categorize it so we can determine how we will treat this situation or person.

There have been labels and identities placed on entire generations. This has been occurring since the mid to late 1800s.

There has been little or NO science applied to developing these labels. The identities by and large have the assessment made by individuals who have given their opinion on what the generation should be called. The generational label that stuck is the one that was embraced.

We then fell into the energy, attitude, behaviors and expectations attached to the generation. As a result, what we see as "normal" for our generation now begins to drive our behavior.

Generation Name	Births Starting	Births Ending	Youngest Age Today	Oldest Age Today (if still alive)
The Lost Generation - The Generation of 1914	1890	1915	101	126
The Interbellum Generation	1901	1913	103	115
The Greatest Generation	1910	1925	91	106
The Silent Generation	1923	1944	72	93
Baby Boomer Generation	1945	1964	52	71
Generation X	1961	1981	35	55
Generation Y - The Millennials - Gen Next	1975	1995	21	41
Generation Z	1995	2015	1	21

* Robinson, M. T. (2017, October 17). "The Generations, Which Generation are You?" Retrieved from careerplanner.com

You will often hear people justifying their behavior by announcing what generational category they embrace. Adhering to this prescribed way of being allows us to fit in or be cool; we do things the way we are supposed to according to the expectations of the paradigm.

Here is the first realization you should understand: every generational distinction was given based on how that generation reacted to the circumstances that were prevalent in their era.

The theory of critical mass says that when 3% of a population begins believing and behaving in a certain way, it will reach critical mass, a shift will occur and the entire population of that group will begin behaving in that manner and consider it normal. You then begin following the crowd and never ask why.

When we do this, we are under-living our potential. I want you to know that normal is mediocrity, it is good nuf', it is playing not to lose. The two things that continue to get lost in these generational categories are Personal Responsibility and Choice. You can choose to be whoever you want to be.

Generation Game Changers know that personal responsibility and choice are the differentiators for greater success, more fulfilled relationships, more successful businesses and careers, healthier lifestyles and so much more. Generation Game Changers are unfazed by circumstances; in fact, they see circumstances as gifts to get stronger. I encourage you to deliberately choose to be a member of Generation Game Changers and choose to make life happen because of you. Let's take it one small step at a time by focusing on accepting personal responsibility for every aspect of our lives and moving forward with the intention of affecting the critical mass in a powerful positive way. #gengc

CHAPTER 5
WHAT IS A WIN?

The first and most significant wins will come with this understanding, the biggest and most sustainable wins will occur in your thinking before any actions are taken. You must believe that what you want is possible before you take the first step.

If your inside doesn't match your outside, you will not be the most effective. What you say you believe must match the conversation you are having with yourself in the moment. That is the only way your actions will produce those results.

What you have been taught and what you say you believe is: Anything is Possible. You have heard this and most of you can parrot it, however, I am asking you to self-examine and look deep within yourself to find your authentic truth regarding this statement. Whether you believe you can or you believe you can't, you are right.

You must also understand that the same mind that got you where you are today, in this moment, will not get you to the next level. Most of you focus on the pain from your past as you say you want to move forward. Be aware that what you focus on will expand. Focusing on your pain and problems will not produce a sustainable solution unless you keep finding pain to resolve or problems to fix. Okay, I know that was incredibly deep, take a moment to understand it before you move forward.

Is Your Past Creating Your Future?

I have a 1:1 coaching client that I will call Greg. Greg is a business owner and he is married with 2 kids. His dad was an abusive alcoholic and Greg vowed to never be like him. He talked about how abusive his dad was and that his dad constantly told him he would never succeed at anything. He always pointed out how weak and sorry Greg was. His dad often told him that he was a loser and Greg observed his dad mentally and physically abusing his mom.

Greg told me that his attitude was "I will show him." Greg's entire focus and driver was committed to prove his dad wrong. He used that pain and negativity as motivation to be successful as a business owner, husband and dad.

That painful, negative driver got him to a certain level of success relative to his experience with his dad; however, it was inadequate to move the needle any farther in a positive way. Greg struggled to maintain where he was and was unable to get to the next level. The relationships with his wife and children were deteriorating because he was no longer driven or motivated to improve these relationships. He said to me, "I have lost my drive, my hunger, my swag, my mojo and my passion to get to my next level."

> *The biggest and most sustainable wins will occur in your thinking before any actions are taken.*

Oh my goodness, there are so many of you that need to hear this; if pain, anger, resentment, or frustration is your driver, you may have some successes, however, unless some more pain, anger, resentment, or frustration shows up, you will not be able to sustain the success or experience any greater success. When the negative, painful energy was no longer an adequate motivator or driver for Greg, he had nothing to push him. If you practice "not to lose", you will play "not to lose". My coaching to him and to you is to identify what you are committed to fight for, rather than what you are committed to fight against. Running to gain is more rewarding than running from pain. Wow, I hope you got that. I don't care who you are, that is Smokin' Hottt.

Your thinking is not the ultimate enemy; however, the source of your thinking could be your greatest enemy. If your thinking is focused on historical events (good or bad) it is the enemy to moving forward and getting to your next level. It is important you understand that the answer to "How can I get to my next level?" will always be historical and never provide an answer that will get you there. How can you think through your problems when your thoughts are the problem? Your thoughts are what you believe the truth is, and as a human being you behave in accordance to that truth. Your truth is where your limitations, fears, self-image and beliefs about what is possible reside.

Absence of Your Truth is Freedom

That truth is the result of everything you have learned and experienced from other human beings. In Greg's case, it came from his dad and mom. Much like Greg, you are either fighting to prove what you were taught and experienced is the truth, or you are fighting to prove that it is not the truth.

The negative situation may be a good initial energy to get you going in the right direction to prove someone wrong, however, it must switch from running from pain or what you don't want, to a focus on gain, or what you do want. You must transform the negative energy to positive energy. Again, I don't care who you are, that is a Smokin' Hottt awareness.

Greg asked me during one of our 1:1 coaching sessions, "How could I possibly know if my decisions are being driven by pain or gain?" What an incredibly powerful question. When you connect to this, everything in your life will change. Read the next few paragraphs with the intention of being influenced to approach everything in your life in this manner.

How can you know beyond any shadow of a doubt that the choice you made is the correct choice for you? How can you be absolutely sure that the direction you just chose is the perfect direction? How can you be 100% certain the behavior you are demonstrating is perfect for the outcome you committed to manifest? You must know where you are going. The only way to know where you are going is to have a specific, positive outcome.

Most of you will set these outcomes focused on instant gratification. As with everything, I believe that instant gratification has a positive and a negative context. If the instant gratification is not leading to a greater success, it is likely unhealthy. If it is leading to an ultimate gratification bigger than the momentarily small satisfaction you are experiencing in the moment, it is likely a healthy gratification and you are on the right path.

You Really Have No Clue

Let's take it a step farther. How many productive years of life do you believe you have left? Some of you will say I have no clue and that is true; you could be gone tomorrow. Why do you believe those are the number of productive years you have left?

Now I want you to look at how you are presently approaching life, professionally, personally, relationally, financially, spiritually, and physically. Will your present approach in these areas of your life get you to where you want to be?

I suppose the real question to ask in this moment is where do you want to be in every one of these areas of your life? What is the optimal outcome you want in every one of these areas of your life? Have you even taken the time to ask or answer those questions? I know some of you have been taught to establish a 3-5 year plan, much like my wife presented to me six years ago. However, I want to push beyond your normal or reasonable, as I did hers.

What if you projected yourself to the end of your life, what do you want to have accomplished in each of those areas by the end of your life?

Okay, let's get real. None of us know how much life we have remaining. We do not know how much time we have left on this earth. What we do know is that we have right now and whatever choices I am making right now is a pen stroke in the story that is being written about me. I convinced Susan that the opportunity for us to create the future we said we wanted was right now.

Put Up or Shut Up

In late Summer of 2006, I was preparing for a trip to Atlanta to conduct a program for one of the teams I was working with.

It was customary for me to get up at 3:30 a.m. and head to Memorial Park for a run. On this day, that is exactly what I did. Less than a tenth of a mile into my run, I was sweating profusely. This was a little unusual for me. I had been dealing with heart issues since I was 22 years old and knew this was a problem. I completed my 3-mile run, went home and showered, and had breakfast at my favorite breakfast restaurant. Then I drove myself to the emergency room. I had been through the emergency room protocol several times over the years so I knew what to expect. I figured if I could get in there and go through all of the tests, I would still have time to catch my flight to Atlanta the next day to conduct my training class.

The ER staff took me through the tests to check my heart to determine if I was having a heart attack. After over 8 hours of tests, they determined I was not having a heart event. The ER doctor contacted my cardiologist, Dr. Lozano, who was on vacation and told him the results. Dr. Lozano, who had worked with me for many years, said he was very uncomfortable with the results and asked them to keep me over night. He said that he would come in from his vacation to take me into the CAT lab in the morning. Let me be clear, he was not only my doctor for many years, he had become my friend.

He arrived early that morning and came into my room and said, "I was afraid that if they let you out of here it would be hard to get you back after my vacation." He went on to explain that the reason this worried him is because I had never experienced this during one of my runs before.

Dr. Lozano took me into the CAT lab and less than 10 minutes later looked at me as I laid awake observing the procedure on two

TV monitors above my feet and said, "We need to go to surgery and we need to go now."

Since it was first determined that I had heart disease, I have been in the CAT lab many times. During this invasive procedure, they enter my body through a vein in my groin with a catheter and snake it through to the chambers of my heart. Once there, they can clearly see what is going on in that moment.

My response to Dr. Lozano was, "Let's go." As they prepped me for surgery, I was overcome with emotion as all the "what ifs" were going through my head. What if I was never able to see my boys again, what if I never had another opportunity to interact with my team members and friends, what if I had given my last speech, what if I would never see my family again, what if I had written my last book, what if I never had another opportunity to love again.

They took me to surgery and I was there for several hours. When I woke up a day later, they informed me they had performed a quintuple open-heart by-pass surgery. I had never heard of such a thing. I had often heard of quadruple by-passes; however, I never knew they did 5 arteries.

When they finally took me to a room and allowed me to have visitors, people came in sad and weeping. When I asked them what was wrong, they said to me "You must not know the seriousness of the surgery you just had."

My response was, "I absolutely know how serious this is, it is another opportunity for me to prove once again that what happens to you does not define you. The choices you make in relation to what happens to you are what define you." A few weeks later I chose to win the moment by announcing that I would be running the Houston Marathon and in January 2008, I successfully accomplished that amazing outcome. Man, I just cried again while recalling that moment.

How Much Longer Do You Have?

What commitments are you willing to make to optimize however many productive years you have remaining on this earth? What happens to you will not define you, how you react or respond to what happens to you will.

Realize that the choice you just made in this moment could have been your last. There literally are people that are over half way through their lives and they don't even know it. This has nothing to do with how old they are. There are people in this present moment that are at the end of their lives and they don't even realize it, and again, it has nothing to do with their age.

Are the choices you are making right now winning the moment to create the outcomes you want in your relationships? What legacy do you want to leave with your significant other when you are gone? Is the way you are treating that person right now creating that positive, supportive, intimate, loving relationship? What would you like for your children to say about the mother or father you were when you are gone? Have you been or are you being the person creating that relationship right now for them to see you as their hero now, and when you are gone?

The only way to know if you are winning the moment is you

must know your outcome, intention and purpose. When you do, you know if the thoughts you are having, the actions you are taking and the words you are speaking are appropriate or inappropriate. You know if your choices, energy, and actions are trending you to your outcomes. You know you are creating your *Win the Moment* legacy.

WIN THE MOMENT

CHAPTER 6
BE SELFISH

Quite often "selfish" is contextualized as a negative. The definition found during several on-line searches is: lacking consideration for others; concerned chiefly with one's own personal profit or pleasure.

The first point that needs to be made here can be applied to every aspect of your life. In EVERYTHING in the universe, there is a positive context and a negative context. Positive and negative cannot exist separate of each other. In every given moment when you are experiencing positive or negative, know that both exist in every moment because they are a comparison to each other.

The only way I can assess something as positive is by comparing it to something that would be assessed as negative. Conversely, for me to assess something as negative, I must compare it to something that I would consider positive.

I believe that the context of everything we are taught during our formative years is the context that is socially agreed on.

From some perspectives, I am assessed as self-confident; from other perspectives, I am assessed as arrogant. From some perspectives, I may be assessed as kind, gentle and considerate; from another perspective, I may be assessed as weak.

The perspectives we were taught have created our truth and we behave in accordance to that truth as we make our life choices. We then manage ourselves and others based on that context as if it is the only truth that exists.

We see positive and negative as good and evil. We teach that positive and negative represent a win/lose in the relationships we have with others, as well as the relationship we have with ourselves.

When we or others make choices outside the context of what we were taught as positive, we mistakenly see that as negative behavior.

Count Your Blessings

When we count our blessings, we count the things that we consider positive. So, the way you look at everything matters. When circumstances happen and you look at them as bad, wrong, unfair or negative, you will not see them as blessings and it will negatively affect how you choose to resolve the circumstances.

Understand that in the moment the circumstance is occurring, positive and negative both exist. When you change the way you look at a circumstance, then the circumstance you are looking at will change. Now I don't care who you are, that is some Smokin' Hottt Shit.

A circumstance is a circumstance. Hurricane Harvey happened at the same time for millions of people, it did not discriminate against anyone. The reality that everyone experienced was the result of how they looked at and assessed the circumstance.

There are some terrible situations that will occur, many of which we have NO control over. If you approach them in negative energy, you will not get to the best resolve.

It is important to have positive outcomes regarding your health, finances, relationships, and your children. It is important to do everything you can to reach those outcomes; however, you cannot have an attachment to them. No matter how it ultimately turns out, count your blessings.

If you are fighting to hold on to something that does not want to be held on to, you may want to let it go. The blessing in it may be about to expire.

If you are counting your blessings and you did not include the things that you considered negative, wrong, bad or unfair in your count, then you are miscounting your blessings. When you change the way you look at life, the life you are looking at will change. So take a recount on those blessings.

Only Your Thinking Makes It So

You were likely raised by adults who agreed with the negative context of being selfish, and so it is the only context you were taught. These adults formed their belief systems on what they learned from other human beings or experiences they encountered. They could only pass down the knowledge they received regarding how to look at things, how to determine good from bad, what is positive versus negative.

For many of you the lack of self-fulfillment you experience is because you see selfish in a negative context. You continue to wait for others to deliver on expectations you have and in many cases, they are not even aware of your expectations.

I do not believe that selfish is negative or selfless is positive; it depends on your perspective. I believe they are dichotomies.

A dichotomy is defined as a division or contrast between two things that are represented as being opposed or entirely different. I believe that your present determining factor of positive and negative is your way of thinking. I submit there is a positive and negative context to selfish and a positive and negative context to selfless. I believe that both can be a strength and both can be a weakness. Is it possible to know when you are being selfish or selfless? How can you possibly know what context is appropriate and when to apply it? I am so glad you asked; the answer will be presented in due time.

You Can't Give Away Something You Don't Have

A theory created by Abraham Maslow that addresses the positive context of selfish is referred to as self-actualization. He states, self-actualization represents growth of an individual toward fulfillment of their highest needs. Specifically, needs that address the meaning of life. Maslow's hierarchy is described as follows:

1. Physiological needs, such as needs for food, sleep and air.

2. Safety or the needs for security and protection.

3. Belonging and love.

4. Needs for self-esteem, self-respect, and healthy, positive feelings derived from admiration.

5. And "being" needs concerning creative self-growth, engendered from fulfillment of potential and meaning in life.

This is the positive selfish foundation each of us need in order to be fulfilled in life. You must understand that you cannot be selfless in a positive context, until you have been selfish in a positive context. The simplest way for me to explain this to you is, you cannot give away something you do not have. If you do not own it or possess it, you cannot give it to someone else.

If you are not living a healthy life style and you are not taking care of yourself, it is just an illusion that you are taking care of someone else in a healthy way. If you are not safe and secure, you cannot provide those things to someone else. If you do not love yourself, feel good about yourself, it is just an illusion that you can truly love someone else or make them feel good about themselves. This belief is one of the foundational philosophies taught in our programs at Discover Leadership Training.

> *If you are counting your blessings and you did not include the things you considered negative in your count, then you are miscounting your blessings.*

YODO

After learning the above truth during one of our experiential processes conducted in the 4-day Master Graduate Leadership Program we facilitate at Discover Leadership Training, a young man that was a participant in the class started saying something on day three of the program that made no sense to me at all. He kept saying YOLO, (pronounced YōLō). I asked the members of my staff if they had a clue what that meant and none of them knew.

Every chance he got he would walk by one of the staff and said, "YOLO" and smiled. I heard of a lot of acronyms: LOL, TTYS, BRB, BTW, ILY, JK, and BYOB, however, I never heard of YOLO.

On day four of the training, he came by even more often and said, "YOLO" then smiled at us. It really started to feel a little creepy. Even still, I did not want to ask him what it meant. After all, I was the guru and this young man was 23 years old; I should know these things, right? I've come to realize, and have been reminded often, there is always an opportunity to learn something new and grow as a result.

I finally gave in and asked him what does "YOLO" mean? He replied, "You Only Live Once". Wow, I was so glad I asked for the definition because I got an opportunity to win that moment by completely changing his paradigm. The gift he set in motion offered each of us the opportunity to change our perspective regarding a common phrase into something that has even more meaning and depth.

I am sure you have heard ministers preach and motivational speakers encourage you and others to live your life full out because you only live once. I do not ascribe to that theory. I believe you have an opportunity to make the choice to live 86,400 times today. What is remarkable about my theory is you are at choice in every one of those moments to choose to live. In reality, you only die once. The next time the young man walked by, I said, "YODO" and smiled. He asked, "What does YODO mean?" and I responded, "You Only Die Once."

WIN THE MOMENT

CHAPTER 7
DEFINING MOMENTS

We have all had what I refer to as "defining moments" occur in our lives. Many times people use the defining moments that happened to them to construct a puzzle, with no picture or reference to what the completed puzzle looks like. They attempt to understand how something that happened to them fits into their life and what meaning it has to defining who they are or what purpose the event has on who they want to become.

We often have expectations about how things should turn out in our lives. Many times those expectations are unfulfilled. When we experience an unfulfilled expectation we see it as wrong, negative, unfair, or bad. As a result, the unfulfilled expectation has a negative effect on our development. When our expectations are fulfilled, we see those as positive defining moments.

Some of your defining moments occurred when you were in grade school; perhaps you raised your hand to answer a question and got it wrong and all the little kids laughed at you. You made a commitment to yourself in that moment to allow that incident to define how you would behave in future moments. Now when the opportunity comes along for you to offer your opinion, you have a defining moment in your memory from school that dictates how you react in the present. Your choice in most situations will be to keep your opinion to yourself.

Some of you early in your life had a crush on a little girl or a little boy and they rejected you. That defining moment for many of you shaped how you feel about yourself and how you approach people you are interested in having a relationship with personally and professionally today. Maybe you were the last to be picked on someone's team. Many of you allowed that defining moment to determine your self-worth and value.

This is Not a Hardwire

You have allowed these defining moments to shape and mold who you are today. Our personality traits come from these moments; introvert versus extrovert, high level of self-confidence or a lack of self-confidence, shy or outgoing, risk-taker or someone who plays it safe.

The defining moments in your life have created who you are. None of you were born into the world with a hardwire, or a predisposition of who you would become. Defining moments, both positive and negative, have created the person you are today.

Recently, there was a gentleman in one of our Master Graduate Leadership Programs (MGLP) that completed the first block of training. At the end of most blocks, each participant writes down the benefits they received from the activities in that block.

After the trainer explained the writing process to the class, this gentleman packed up all of his belongings and left the room.

I was standing in the break room right outside the class room and I asked him where he was going. He had his back pack on and appeared to be leaving. He said he was illiterate and could not write. He went on to say that his boss knew he could not write and should have informed him that writing would be part of the training process. He said if he had known, he would not have attended the training. His boss was a graduate of the MGLP and clearly did not inform him there would be writing and yet, wanted him to attend the program because of the personal benefits he would receive.

I asked this gentleman if that was the only reason he was quitting and he replied that it was. I told him that should be the last reason he leaves because when you are on a team and you run into a wall or one of your limitations, the team will pick you up. I told him that it does not make you weak to ask others for help and if he had the courage to push through his fears of asking for help and continue the training, there would come a time during this 4-day tough program that someone else would run into their limitations or wall and would need his help.

He made the choice to stay and ask for help. His team picked him up and helped him complete each of his journals. When opportunities arose for someone to stand and read aloud in the classroom, he pushed past his fears, stood up and read out loud. He became aware that no one would judge him. His team was there to help him be successful. There came several times when this gentleman had an opportunity to pick up another team member and he was there for them. The ultimate benefit he received from understanding it is okay to ask for help, allowed him to get the full benefits of the 4-day program. I asked him at the end of the program if it was worth pushing through his fears of remaining in the training and he responded with a resounding, "Yes, it completely changed my life."

Somebody had convinced this gentleman early in his life that he was dumb, that he was illiterate, and he experienced defining moments where he got evidence this was true. Believing that story prevented him from pushing through his fears.

When opportunities came up in his life and he chose not to read or write, he was simply reinforcing what he already believed the truth to be and was not creating a new possibility. We get really good at what we practice, so every time he practiced not reading or writing he got better at convincing himself that he was illiterate.

When he won that moment during the training, he created a new defining moment. He became aware that he could read and write better than he thought. He could clearly see an improvement in his reading and writing by getting out of his comfort zone and allowing himself to be vulnerable during the four days of the Master Graduate Leadership Program.

What or Who has Defined You?

What defining moments occurred in your life that are still perpetuating your fears and limitations? Was it an experience, or something someone you gave value to said about you, and you bought it?

Create an opportunity for you to win the moment. Deliberately put yourself in a situation where you can reframe the defining moment and create a positive outcome.

When I was in the seventh grade I went out for the football team. I made the cut and this was the first time I played a competitive sport. The coach had me playing offense and defense on the eighth grade team. We went through the entire season without losing a game and I became very familiar with what it felt like to win, however, I had no clue what it felt like to lose.

> *Defining moments, both positive and negative, have created the person you are today.*

Our eighth grade team made it to the championship game and we lost. I did not know what to do in that moment; I cried like a baby. I felt hurt and disappointed. In that defining moment, I became aware that I did not like losing. That defining moment shaped a lot of things for me as it relates to my work ethic and preparation for everything I do.

Every defining moment has a positive and a negative story attached to it. Being rejected as an adolescent could define you as a loser. Accepting that was not the right person or time for you, dusting yourself off, and going for it again and again and again until you succeed, could define you as a winner.

I absolutely believe you must set specific outcomes and you should go for them with your heart, body and soul. I absolutely believe that the picture in your mind should be of your imminent success; however, I do not believe you should have an attachment to the outcome.

Recognize that if you choose to play at this level, there will be instances when you will fail. The moment failure occurs is when you get to define the moment and not have the moment define you. Failures will be a part of the authentication process. Whether you succeed or fail, my coaching is to not have an attachment to the outcome. Also, whether you succeed or fail, I suggest you have a short memory.

Celebrate or grieve for a short period of time and then get on with it. Trend progression is time that will work for you or against you. The longer you celebrate a victory or failure, you are creating space that must be overcome to get to the next start.

Think about a championship team who takes a year off. There will be an incredible deficit to overcome to get back into championship form in order to be victorious again. Or consider a salesperson that celebrates a big sale for too long and spends all of their commission in the celebration. If they don't go back to work and look for the next sale, the longer it will take to find.

Time to Surrender

Identify defining moments in your life. There was always a universal conspiracy going on that was focused on your success. Whatever has happened to you does not have to become you.

Look back at those defining moments and look now through a different lens; how can you reframe what happened in a positive way? How can you use the circumstance that occurred in your life to write a new story that allows you to create a better version of yourself? Would you rather remain bitter or get better? Throw up the white flag.

Most of you feel that throwing up the white flag means you quit. Many of you feel that to surrender is weak, however, not in this context.

Giving in, in this context, does not mean giving up. My coaching to you is to create a discontent for where you are and surrender to it. The only way you will get stronger and create an even better version of yourself is to surrender.

Creating discontent does not mean that you are dissatisfied, or that something is wrong or broken. Creating a discontent can also mean you are satisfied and are choosing to move to your next level.

There doesn't need to be a frown on your face before you decide you are ready for the next adventure in your life; you do not need to run away from something to move from where you are; you don't need to be told that you are dying before you choose to LIVE.

To surrender does not mean you are weak. Surrendering means that you have been awakened to the fact that you do not need to assess something to be wrong, bad, negative or a failure for you to take action now to get to your next level in every area of your life.

When you surrender, you will become aware there is more to life than you have experienced; that you are worthy of an even happier, more fulfilled life in every aspect.

WIN THE MOMENT

No matter what happens in the next moment, rather than allowing the moment to define you, I encourage you to define the moment, own it, and make it what you want it to be.

CHAPTER 8
I CAN'T AFFORD IT!

In Chapter 5 we talked about the phrase "Anything is Possible". Though many of us repeat those words and tell our children this phrase, when we are faced with something we do not have the full capacity or resources to make happen, we often resign to a belief we can't have that thing or we settle for something less than what we really, really wanted.

Now I know, "anything is possible" was taught to you, however, if you authentically believed it, you would never say "I can't afford it, I can't do that, I am too old, I am not good enough, I am not tall enough, or that's not me."

In my book *Unreasonable Possibilities*, I talked about how the conversation we have with ourselves leads to our behaviors because your energy and actions will follow your thoughts and as a "human doing" you behave in accordance to what you authentically believe to be true. Whatever moment you are in is won or lost based on what you truly believe the truth is.

When you create a conversation that declares any of the "I Can't Afford It" affirmations, you are saying that impossible exists and you really do not feel that what you want is available to you. If you were committed to and believed you really wanted it, and a "But I can't afford it" statement follows, then you actually avow you are not worth having what you say you want. If you really believe you are worth having it, then you are saying that you are not committed to make it happen, which ultimately means you really do not believe you can have it and therefore, you are not worth it.

When you have a conversation with yourself that "I can't afford it", you narrow your vision. As you view what you believe is possible through this tunnel vision, the vast resources available to you cannot be seen.

In Chapter 3 of my book entitled *Change Your Mind, Change Your World*, I talked about the difference between the flag and the wind. This flag and the wind concept is SO big that I talk about it in every keynote I conduct. When you fully grasp the message and embrace its meaning, it will be transformative in the way you approach living your life moving forward.

There was a gentleman that heard me speak several times and asked, "Why do you mention the flag and the wind in all of your presentations?" I responded by telling him a story.

There was a young minister seeking an appointment to be the pastor for a church. The church congregation had brought in several ministers to determine who would be their next pastor. The young man preached a powerful, moving message during his opportunity. The church elders gathered to determine which of these ministers they would offer the appointment as their next pastor. It was unanimously decided that the young minister would be their next pastor.

The young man was notified of their decision and arrived the following Sunday as the pastor. As he took the pulpit to deliver the sermon, he preached the exact same sermon as he did the first time he stood before them. The very next Sunday he preached the exact same sermon again.

The elders of the church became concerned that he only had one sermon and pulled him aside and said, "Pastor, that is a very powerful sermon, with a powerful message, however, we have heard it a few times. Do you have any other sermons?" He responded, "Absolutely, I have quite a few sermons that I believe are just as powerful as this sermon. I decided that I would move on to those as soon as you all get this one."

Truly embracing the message of the flag and the wind will push up against what you have been taught, however, when you fully understand it, you will know that the best possible life you can live is more available to you when you embrace this simple, yet, profound concept.

The first question you must ask yourself is, "Am I the flag or am I the wind?"

The flag is passive; it sits around waiting for an energy to show up to give it direction. The flag always moves in the direction of the biggest energy, the flag is waiting for permission to take action. The flag accepts no responsibility to control its direction. The flag will go where it is told to go and will do what it is told to do. The flag will only have what the wind gives it. It will only grow to the level someone else lifts it.

The wind is deliberate, it is purposeful. The wind provides the energy that determines direction, speed, and the ebbs and flows. The wind makes a statement and it is bold. The wind is creative and adventurous.

When you say, "I can't afford it", you are being the flag, waiting for something to happen to you in order for you to receive the things in life you say you want. When you say, "I can't afford it", you have lost the moment.

There might be times when you choose to be the flag and wait for something or someone to show up and provide you with the resources you need. That may have worked for you intermittently, however, the next time you have a need, you likely will not be able to replicate that success unless your winning strategy to have someone else do it for you manifests every time.

Whatever you want is available to you, no matter how large or small. Anything really is possible; however, you must believe it before you see it. That will be your first win.

If you have a conversation with yourself that says, "keep your outcome realistic", be aware where your definition of unrealistic begins is where your belief in what is possible ends. Now I don't care who you are, that is a Smokin' Hottt, eye-opening awareness. When you identify something as unrealistic, the only thing that you have authentically identified is your incapacity to believe beyond what you can see or what you presently possess the resources to obtain.

As soon as you say, "I can't afford it", you give ALL of the negative forces in the universe permission to work against you like a category 5 hurricane. It provides permission to bring every barrier and obstacle in your way to prove you are right, that you really can't afford it.

An "I can't afford it" attitude is clearly not just about money. It is a creed that permeates throughout a person's entire belief system. I had a young high school client that was a swimmer. He was told by his coach that because of his height, he would never be able to swim above certain times in his events. He believed this coach who basically taught him that he could not afford it. The coach sold this young man on the belief he did not have the resources, talents, gifts or the possibility of being an amazingly successful swimmer because of his size.

Anything really is possible; however, you must believe it before you see it. That will be your first win.

Well, he was not likely going to grow several more inches and quite frankly that was outside of his control. However, there were a few very powerful things within his control that were game changers. I believe that game changers are those things and people that alter a predictable negative future in a positive way. I further believe most of the things that fit into that category are within your control.

As a result of the young man believing he did not have the resources to swim those times, he behaved in accordance to that erroneous truth and therefore empowered every negative force that was available to keep him from reaching that outcome.

When you do this, you make "Murphy's Law" a reality; anything that could possibly go wrong, will go wrong.

After he attended our breakthrough leadership training, I began coaching him at his dad's request. He had a tough time believing he could afford it, that he could swim faster times with the body he had.

I taught him how to set a very specific outcome he was committed to and then developed a list of meaningful benefits he would receive after reaching that outcome. We determined the time frame to reach his outcome and decided who his accountability partner would be.

Our next focus was to take the first step necessary to get a quick win, with the understanding that every coin has two sides. I informed him that I did not embrace Murphy's Law, instead Discover Leadership Training had established our own law that says **anything that could possibly go right, will go right**. This young man became aware that both of these beliefs were available to him and that he could choose either of them in every given moment. This is true for you as well.

Quite often individuals attempt to go directly from A to Z without taking the steps necessary to get there. Taking the step necessary to win the moment to get you to "B" successfully helps you break old patterns and develop behaviors that can be replicated as you get a quick win. That quick win will also allow you to build the self-confidence needed to take the next step and incrementally get to a bigger win.

He continued living these principles and following this process and as a result, improved his times and his successes. He eventually received a full scholarship to a prestigious university, which was his outcome and additionally, he became the captain of the university's swim team. The same principles and processes we are practicing in our 30-day challenge from Chapter 2 are the principles and processes I have used to help students, business owners and executives from all over the world win the moment. Apply these principles to prove that you can afford it.

- Identify what you want by setting an outcome and make a commitment to that outcome. Buy a business, increase sales, improve your relationship, get physically healthier, get a promotion, improve your grades, or get a better job.

- Develop seven very meaningful benefits you will receive when you reach your outcome. These benefits should have some emotion attached to them. The benefits should be things that will make a positive, significant impact on your life and on the lives of others.

- Determine what your time frame will be. Once you have determined your time frame to reach your outcome, I recommend you establish some shorter time frames or milestones to be able to observe your trending and to give yourself something to hold yourself accountable.

- Identify someone you have a trusting relationship with and share your outcome with them. It will be important to give them permission to hold you accountable to do what you said you would do.

- Have the courage to take the first step to make the outcome your reality. Once you understand what you want, ask yourself repeatedly, what am I committed to do in this present moment to get to my outcome. What am I committed to do to win the moment?

As soon as you have identified this step it may be very scary, however, I want you to know that courage is not absent of fear. Real courage is acknowledging the fear, remaining focused on your outcome and your meaningful benefits and taking the step in spite of the fear. That is the moment you must win in order to get to your outcome. Think about this for just one moment, what is the worst thing that could happen when you take that step? You could fail, you could drop the ball. So what? Remember, winners lose more often than losers, lose. If you fail, get up, dust yourself off, get refocused on your outcome and get yourself back in the game. If you drop the ball, learn what you need to from that situation, pick that ball up and move your butt.

Discover Leadership Training had established our own law that says anything that could possibly go right, will go right.

If my outcome is to get a promotion this year, as soon as I establish the outcome, I contextualize the appropriate positive conversation that I will create with myself. The appropriate, positive energy and actions will follow that conversation.

The first thing I would do at that point is go to the person who would ultimately determine my state of readiness for the position I am focused on obtaining and have that person make me aware of all the skills and attributes they are looking for in the position. Then I believe it is critical for you to determine how they feel you stack up in this moment and what areas they believe you need to work on to be the person selected for the position. It is important to be able to see yourself through their eyes.

Once you are armed with this information, if you are still focused on the outcome of being promoted to that position in the next 12 months, then it is time to make a commitment to Just do WIT (Whatever It Takes) to make it happen. As soon as you make that commitment the resources you need will come into view as you realize all you need to do today is 100% of what is available to you. You must understand every journey begins with the first step and the appropriateness of every step is authenticated based on the outcome you set.

Now, at this point most people would sit down and craft out a plan. If that is your preference then go for it, however, I believe that crafting a plan in this situation will bring in limitations to what is available. If you come up with a plan, it will be historical in nature, based on things you have done in the past or someone else's opinion of how you should approach it based on their past successes or failures. I am of the opinion this approach is playing 'not to lose' and will not distinguish you from the crowd, because most of them will use this same safe approach.

If you want to potentially create something really special, then I recommend the only plan you have is to "be in the moment" and make the choice to *Win the Moment.*

You know what your outcome is, and you made a commitment to make it happen. I suggest you craft seven very meaningful benefits you will receive from obtaining this promotion. Then continually live every moment asking yourself, "What am

I committed to do today to take the next step to get to my outcome?"

I recommend you do what I refer to as "mental reps" where you project yourself to the outcome, create in your mind what it will feel like to arrive at that outcome. See yourself experiencing the benefits of the outcome.

Now let's not call this "meditation" or have you feel like you need to get "Zen like" by sitting with your legs crossed and your eyes closed. When you are performing a "mental rep" you can keep your eyes wide open. My coaching is that you get somewhere quiet for a few short minutes.

What you have now done is endowed all of the powers of the universe to help you see the incredible opportunities and resources available to you to make your outcome a reality. You will literally be able to see yourself trending to your outcome as you become aware that everything in the universe is conspiring for your success and anything that can possibly go right, will go right. You must believe it is possible before you execute. The very first win is going to occur in your thinking.

When you choose to approach the things you want using these powerful principles and processes, you will experience greater successes in both your personal and professional life. Living life "in the moment" takes practice and it is simple, however, not always easy. Commit to do the work, focus on your outcome and benefits, and surround yourself with people who will hold you accountable and support you. You are worth it. You deserve it. Now go out and make every moment count. *Win the Moment.*

I CAN'T AFFORD IT!

www.ingramcontent.com/pod-product-compliance
Lightning Source LLC
Chambersburg PA
CBHW032050090426
42744CB00004B/147